jB
CASSIDY

Stewart, Gail B.,
   1949-

Where lies Butch
   Cassidy?

$11.95

DATE			

8.93

BAKER & TAYLOR BOOKS

WHERE LIES
BUTCH CASSIDY?

by

Gail B. Stewart

Illustrated by
Yoshi Miyaki

CRESTWOOD HOUSE
NEW YORK

Maxwell Macmillan Canada
Toronto

Maxwell Macmillan International
New York   Oxford   Singapore   Sydney

Library of Congress Cataloging-in-Publication Data
Stewart, Gail B., 1949-

    Where lies Butch Cassidy? / by Gail B. Stewart. — 1st ed.
      p. cm. — (History's mysteries)
    Includes bibliographical references and index.
    Summary: Presents a biography of the famous rustler and outlaw, and discusses the mystery surrounding his death.
    ISBN 0-89686-618-1
    1. Cassidy, Butch, b. 1866—Death and burial—Juvenile literature. 2. Outlaws—West (U.S.)—Biography—Juvenile literature. 3. Crime—West (U.S.)—History—Juvenile literature. 4. West (U.S.)—History—1848–1950—Juvenile literature. 5. Cassidy, Butch, b. 1866. [1. Robbers and outlaws.] I. Title. II. Series.
    F595.C362S74 1992
    364.1'55'092—dc20
    [B]   91-25368
                                                     CIP
                                                       AC

Crestwood House
Macmillan Publishing Company
866 Third Avenue
New York, NY 10022

Maxwell Macmillan Canada, Inc.
1200 Eglinton Avenue East
Suite 200
Don Mills, Ontario M3C 3N1

Macmillan Publishing Company is part of the Maxwell Communication Group of Companies.

First edition

Printed in the United States of America

10 9 8 7 6 5 4 3 2 1

CONTENTS

▲▲▲▲▲▲▲▲▲▲▲▲▲▲▲▲▲▲▲▲▲▲▲▲▲▲▲▲▲▲▲▲▲

THE CASE OPENS

▲▲▲▲▲▲▲▲▲▲▲▲▲▲▲▲▲▲▲▲▲▲▲▲▲▲▲▲▲▲

Sometimes the man called himself Jim Ryan or Billy Maxwell or something else. He made different combinations of all his names too, using one first name with various last names. Sometimes he spelled one of his names LeRoy and sometimes it was Leroy. Seldom did he use his real name— Robert Leroy Parker. He didn't want to bring shame on his family.

Most people at the turn of the 20th century knew him as Butch Cassidy. They had seen his face on WANTED posters throughout the West. They knew he was a rustler and an outlaw. They knew that Butch and his partner, Harry Longabaugh— known as the Sundance Kid—were part of an infamous gang called the Wild Bunch.

With others of his gang, Butch Cassidy robbed banks and trains of more than $500,000. But except for a short stay in a Wyoming prison for cattle rustling at the age of 28, he was never arrested for his crimes.

Butch Cassidy was also well-known for something else uncommon for a criminal—his good-hearted nature. When pursued by posses, he shot at the horses, never at the riders. He said, apparently truthfully, "I have never killed a man."

Historians agree. Cassidy was one of the few Western outlaws who never had "killed" or "murdered" on his WANTED posters.

Like his life, Butch Cassidy's death was legendary. By 1906, Cassidy and the Sundance Kid were being pursued by lawmen from Montana to the Mexican border. To keep from being captured and hanged for their crimes, the two fled to South America.

In 1908, word reached American law officials that the outlaws had been killed by a regiment of Bolivian soldiers. The bodies of Cassidy and the Sundance Kid were identified by several Bolivian authorities as well as by Percy Seibert, a man who had become their friend.

When word of the deaths reached the United States, officials there stopped their investigations. Cassidy and the Sundance Kid, who over the years had been hunted by more than 1,000 lawmen, were hunted no longer.

The American public learned the exciting details of the outlaws' deaths 20 years later, in 1930. Arthur Chapman wrote a vivid account of the incident for *Elks Magazine*.

Cassidy and Sundance were surrounded by heavily armed soldiers, Chapman wrote. Bullets whistled through windows, and blood from the shooting settled in "little pools about the courtyard."

His account ended with the soldiers surrounding the outlaws who were trapped in a small house near the courtyard. The soldiers heard two shots fired late in the evening and then nothing more until noon the following day.

When the soldiers finally stormed the little house, they found Cassidy and Sundance dead. "Cassidy had fired a bullet into Longabaugh's head," Chapman wrote, "and had used his last cartridge to kill himself."

The Chapman article seemed to be the last word on the famous Butch Cassidy. Scholars and historians quoted Chapman when they wrote about the death of the outlaw. In fact, in *Outlaw Trail*, one of the most widely read histories of the Old West,

author Charles Kelly used Chapman as his source in writing about Cassidy's death. Cassidy's death was a fact—or so it seemed.

The mystery arose in the mid-1930s. Rumors began spreading that Butch Cassidy had not died in Bolivia. According to those rumors, Butch was alive and well in the United States.

Cassidy's relatives in Utah claimed to have spoken with him in the late 1920s. His sister Lula Parker Betenson wrote a book, *Butch Cassidy, My Brother*. In the book she said that Butch visited them at their Utah ranch in 1925. And there he had died after a long illness in 1937.

A different version of Cassidy's death was also circulating. Some Wyoming old-timers reported in the 1930s that a man calling himself William T. Phillips had visited them, and that he was really Butch Cassidy.

The Wyoming state treasurer in 1936 was a man named Mart Christensen. Christensen had records indicating that Cassidy, using the name Phillips, visited the area and spoke to many of his old friends.

Could the "old friends'" have been mistaken about Phillips? Not a chance, according to Christensen. In a 1936 letter to an Old West expert, Christensen wrote, "It would be preposterous to any of the people I have named that they are mistaken. George LeRoy Parker, alias Butch Cassidy—now known as William Phillips, in the state of Washington—was alive six months ago and resides in Spokane."

Many of the facts in this case are conflicting. No one has yet been able to answer questions about the most troubling aspects of Butch Cassidy's death. Did he die in a bloody shoot-out in Bolivia, as many historians claim? If so, why do relatives and friends swear that he had returned from South America? Was William Phillips simply another alias for Butch Cassidy, famous outlaw? Can the answers ever be known?

THE CASE FILE

▲▲▲▲▲▲▲▲▲▲▲▲▲▲▲▲▲▲▲▲▲▲▲▲▲▲▲▲▲▲

SIMPLE BEGINNINGS

In order to solve the mystery of Butch Cassidy's death, it helps to know more about his life. Butch Cassidy was born Robert Leroy Parker in Beaver, Utah, on April 6, 1866—the year after the American Civil War ended. His parents named him after his grandfather Robert Parker, a Mormon who had come to Utah from England in the mid-1800s. To keep from getting the two Robert Parkers confused, the family called the boy Bob, or sometimes Roy.

Bob's father, Maximillian Parker, was a mail carrier, going south daily from Beaver to Sanford Bench, Utah. On his mail route, Maximillian was impressed with the farmland in a valley he passed each day. In 1879 he was able to purchase a homestead of 160 acres, and the family moved from Beaver to the new ranch.

Life for the Parkers was difficult. They had a small herd of cattle and a crop of wheat. Even though life on the Circle Valley ranch was hard, Lula Parker Betenson wrote that their family was a happy, loving one. "It was not all work and no play. Our parents' love of fun was passed on to us children."

SOURED ON JUSTICE

It may seem surprising that a criminal like Butch Cassidy came from a family that was loving and deeply religious, but it is true. What went wrong?

Historians who have studied Butch Cassidy's life point to two episodes that soured him on the fairness of justice and law.

The first occurred when he was 13. He went into town on horseback to buy a new pair of overalls. Bob found the store closed when he got there. As historian Larry Pointer wrote in his book *In Search of Butch Cassidy*, "Rather than make a return trip, Roy let himself into the building, took a pair of jeans, and left a note promising to return later to pay his debt."

Unfortunately for young Bob Parker, the storekeeper was angry about the incident. He went

to the local sheriff and filed a formal complaint against Bob.

The boy was confused. He thought he had done the right thing by leaving an IOU. According to Pointer, Parker "had been raised with the frontier ethic that a man's word was his bond. . . . Before the matter was settled, the humiliated youth was having mixed emotions over legal process and blind justice."

Another incident that added to Bob Parker's distrust of the law involved his father's right to own more property.

During the frigid, snowy winter of 1880, the Parker family lost all but two of their cattle. This was a real setback, and Maximillian Parker decided to homestead more land to grow more wheat.

But the plan failed. After working the land for more than a year, Maximillian lost the land to another settler who claimed the land was his. As was the custom in many Utah towns, a Mormon bishop acted as judge in the case.

Maximillian lost and was bitterly angry. He had always been relaxed about following the church teachings—he smoked, and sometimes he missed worship services. When the bishop ruled against him, he was convinced it was because of these things.

Like his father, young Bob Parker resented the way the homesteading decision had been made. Such resentment might well have soured him further on the ideas of fairness and justice.

LEARNING TO USE THE "LONG ROPE"

Since the family could not homestead more land, some of the Parkers took extra jobs to pay debts. Bob got a job as a ranch hand on the Marshall ranch 12 miles south.

While working there, Bob met an easygoing young man named Mike Cassidy. Cassidy was a master at many of the skills needed by cowboys, including riding and shooting. He took Bob under his wing.

In *Bloodletters and Badmen*, Jay Robert Nash wrote that "Mike taught his young protege how to shoot better that any apprentice outlaw in the territory. Some stories had it that the teenager became so accurate with a six-gun that he could shoot a playing card dead center from fifty paces away."

Cassidy was also good at a dishonest practice called rustling. Rustling meant taking cattle from another rancher's herd and keeping them as one's own. Surprising as it may seem, a little rustling was tolerated in those days.

Most of the largest cattle herds belonged to the wealthy cattle barons. The herds grazed on vast areas of public land. Often, small ranchers just getting started would claim part of that land—as they had a right to.

The ranchers resented the large herds of the cattle barons, just as the barons resented the shrinking area of public grazing land. As a result, there was disagreement between them.

One of the most common ways the small ranchers "got even" with the large cattlemen was by rustling calves without brands. Cowboys in those days used the term "long rope" to mean taking and branding someone else's cattle.

Some cowboys overdid it. Mike Cassidy was one of these, and he gladly taught young Bob Parker the fine tricks of cattle rustling. Bob was a willing pupil. So willing, in fact, that when he set out on his own in 1884, he changed his name to George Cassidy. "George" was a name he had always liked; "Cassidy" was in honor of his hero and teacher.

THE OUTLAW TRAIL

George Cassidy left home, unsure of what he

wanted to be. He was anxious to see more of the world than Utah, so he headed for Wyoming. There he found a variety of jobs.

Sometimes he was a ranch hand; other times he herded cattle. Once he ran a pack train of mules carrying ore out of a mine. For about six months he worked as a butcher—earning the nickname Butch, which he liked even better than George.

Five years after leaving home, Butch met up with Tom and Billy McCarty, two brothers who were in the business of robbing banks and trains. They were likable, and Butch joined their gang.

Tom McCarty, the leader of the gang, had one rule for robbing a bank—always use the finest horses possible. He knew there would be a chase, and with strong, fast horses he and his men usually had no trouble getting away.

In 1889 Butch joined the gang in what was his first major crime—holding up the bank in Telluride, Colorado. They made off with $10,500 in cash. No shots were fired, and no one was hurt. As usual, the lightning-fast McCarty horses easily got away from the town posse.

THE CATTLEMEN TAKE CONTROL

Butch used his share of the holdup money to buy

a small ranch. Like other small ranchers, he did his share of rustling.

But the West in the 1890s was changing. Some of the "long rope" tactics he had learned from Mike Cassidy as a teenager were becoming dangerous. The cattle ranchers had begun fighting off the small ranchers who branded "unclaimed" cattle. Strangely enough, the fighting began because of a drought.

There was almost no rain during the summer of 1886. Because of this, there was little grass growing on the prairie. The huge herds of cattle grew lean and hungry.

That winter, things got even worse. The temperature on the plains dropped to 40 degrees below zero, and then the snow started. Cattle already weak from the summer's drought suffered in the blizzard.

After the drought and blizzard of 1886-1887, the cattle business changed. No longer did the cattlemen tolerate the long ropers. Instead, they paid cowboys extra to guard the herds. Sometimes they even brought in their own "armies" to kill suspected rustlers.

With their armies, the cattle bosses were taking control of the West. No longer was the West an open

frontier, as it had been. As the 19th century hurried to a close, the frontier was controlled by the people with money—the banks, the cattlemen and even the railroads whose tracks carved up the prairie.

PRISON TIME

In 1893, Butch Cassidy was arrested. The charge was rustling calves and a horse. Butch angrily denied the charges. He was convicted, however, and sentenced to two years in the Wyoming State Penitentiary in Rawlins.

The history books say that Butch was a model prisoner. According to his sister, Butch was called into Governor W. A. Richard's office after serving 18 months of his sentence.

The governor agreed to let Cassidy go on one condition—that he promise never to rustle cattle or rob banks in the state of Wyoming. Cassidy agreed, and the two men shook hands on the deal. He was formally released on January 19, 1896.

Butch Cassidy kept his part of the bargain. He never robbed a Wyoming bank, and he never again rustled cattle in that state. As he saw it, he was bound for bigger things.

THE HOLE-IN-THE-WALL

Cassidy's activities after getting out of prison make it hard to believe he wanted to "go straight." The first thing he did was to visit a place he'd heard about in the penitentiary called the Hole-in-the-Wall. It was a hideout for the toughest criminals and outlaws in the West.

The Hole-in-the-Wall was then and is today an isolated valley in northwestern Wyoming. It is a natural formation of rock and land almost hidden from view.

The Hole-in-the-Wall was a perfect place for outlaws to hide because it had only one entrance and exit. Sheriffs and their posses were reluctant to enter the Hole-in-the-Wall. They knew they would be walking into unfamiliar territory where eyes would be watching them every minute.

Butch Cassidy was well liked by many of the men he met at Hole-in-the-Wall. It was from these outlaws that Cassidy started a gang of his own. It was known throughout the West as the Wild Bunch.

THE WILD BUNCH

Some of the gang were wanted for rustling, some

for stealing horses and others for murder.

The leadership was shared by Butch and a dark-complexioned killer named Kid Curry. The Kid had one of the fastest draws of the Wild Bunch and never hesitated to use his gun. He was the planner, the "brains" behind each crime. Butch was the easygoing, smiling one. He could keep the mood light and the men from becoming angry with one another.

No one is certain how many members there were. As James Horan noted in *The Authentic Wild West*, "There were many who appeared briefly, only to disappear when they had made their 'raise.'" However, there was a well-known "core" at the center of the Wild Bunch's activities.

Elza Lay, for example, was nicknamed The Educated Man. He had once studied geology with a professor from Yale, and he enjoyed reading about mining and geology.

Ben "Tall Texan" Kilpatrick, on the other hand, was completely illiterate. He never ordered anything but ham and beans in saloons because he couldn't read the menus to see what else was available.

Tom O'Day was the lookout for the group. When the gang was holding up a bank, Peep, as he was

called, would hold the horses and watch for sheriffs.

Perhaps the most well-known of the Wild Bunch—next to Butch—was Harry Longabaugh. He was usually called the Sundance Kid because he spent his time in jail in Sundance, Wyoming, for horse theft.

Sundance was a handsome blond with a fast draw. He was precise and careful about details. Historian James Horan reported that he even stitched his initials on every piece of clothing he owned—down to his socks and underwear—so it would not get mixed up with anyone else's.

TAKING THE WEST BY STORM

The Wild Bunch stayed together for several years, robbing banks and trains. However, if all the stories about how many crimes the gang committed could be believed, the Wild Bunch robbed banks in three different states on the same day! For this reason, historians are unsure about the gang's activities.

It is known that they held up trains and banks in New Mexico, Utah, Colorado, Montana and Idaho. Most of the time their "jobs" went smoothly and were profitable. Their first holdup, a bank in

Montpelier, Idaho, netted them $30,000 in cash. Another, in New Mexico, gained the gang $37,000.

Often, the gang split the money and spent it quickly. But there are legends about stashes of cash the outlaws made in the rocky hill country.

As the Wild Bunch got more active, the law got more serious. Sheriffs and marshals throughout the West had little success chasing the Wild Bunch. They had to depend on volunteers for posses and deputies. To catch Cassidy and his gang required professionals.

The gang robbed a Union Pacific train in Wyoming. Butch had kept his word to the governor about rustling and banks, but no one had ever mentioned trains. The robbery made railroad officials furious. They hired private detectives from the Pinkerton Agency who were trained in tracking outlaws. Special Pinkerton agents began a round-the-clock search for Cassidy and his gang.

One agent, Charles Siringo, tracked Butch and Sundance for almost four years. At one point, Siringo infiltrated the gang, pretending to be an outlaw himself. He was accepted as part of the Wild Bunch for a while. As part of the gang, Siringo alerted the railroad when he heard a robbery being planned. That way, railroad officials could change large sums of money to a different train.

Siringo's trick worked—at least for a short time. In one robbery, the gang found less than $50 in the safe of a train they thought would be carrying thousands. Thanks to Siringo, the train loaded with more than $100,000 in gold had passed a few hours earlier. Then Cassidy caught on that Siringo was a detective, and the agent had to run for his life.

On one occasion, the gang members themselves helped the Pinkertons. What started as a practical joke almost landed them all in jail.

After robbing the bank in Winnemucca, Nevada, five gang members fled to Fort Worth, Texas. They thought it would be fun to spend their earnings on flashy new clothes. Then they decided to get their pictures taken.

They visited the studio of a professional Fort Worth photographer. The photograph turned out so well that Butch thought it would be fun to send a copy to the Winnemucca bank. They did so, with a note saying, "Thanks for your contribution."

Pinkerton agents traced the photograph to Fort Worth and came within a few hours of catching Cassidy and his men.

NOWHERE LEFT TO HIDE

As the months went by, law enforcement officials grew more frustrated. The Union Pacific Railroad even tried a new tactic—putting special cars on some trains loaded with hired gunmen and their horses.

The gunmen were armed with high-powered rifles and were ready to come charging out of the car at the first hint of trouble. There were a few close calls for Cassidy and his gang, but they still managed to evade the law.

But the Wild Bunch could not go on forever. Their days were numbered, and Cassidy knew it, although some members of the gang did not.

So while some members of the gang continued to search for "more plump" banks to rob, Cassidy and Sundance came up with another plan. They would move to South America. There was homesteading there and open space.

Sundance left first. He and his "ladylove," a former schoolteacher named Etta Place, went to New York. They enjoyed the sights there while they waited for space on a ship to South America. They sailed in 1901. Butch Cassidy joined them the following spring.

DISCOVERED!

One of the bonuses of moving to South America was that Cassidy and Sundance would not be hounded by the Pinkertons. For a while it seemed they could make a fresh start.

The three of them—Cassidy, Sundance and Etta Place—purchased a ranch in Argentina in 1901. They bought cattle, sheep and horses, and registered their purchases with the government land office. They gave the appearance of being law-abiding citizens.

However, in 1903 Pinkerton agents picked up their trail. The agency alerted one of its best detectives, Frank Dimaio, who was already working in South America on another case. Dimaio was told to go to Buenos Aires, Argentina. Once he arrived, he would learn the best way of capturing the outlaws.

But getting from the city of Buenos Aires to an out-of-the-way ranch was a different story. It required a long, difficult journey. It was the rainy season, and the few roads were not passable.

So Dimaio waited. While he waited, he put up WANTED posters everywhere. He talked to business people who bought beef and wool, alerting them to two dangerous outlaws who might be doing business with them.

Word got to Butch and Sundance. They realized they could not hide, not even in this strange new country. It was dangerous to stay on the ranch, for Dimaio would come looking for them. It was time to move on.

But where?

RETURN TO OUTLAWRY

During the next four years, Butch and Sundance returned to robbing banks. Etta Place returned to the United States, although historians aren't sure just why.

The two outlaws used phony names—Butch was Santiago Maxwell and Sundance was Enrique Brown. They got odd jobs at ranches and mines along the way.

In Bolivia they sometimes worked at a large tin mine for Percy Seibert. Seibert learned their real identities, but he told the men he would not turn them in. In a 1961 interview with historian James Horan, Seibert said that he and Cassidy became friends.

THE END?

In the winter of 1908, the official search for Butch and Sundance ended.

Two men identified as the outlaws were killed in a gun battle with a unit of Bolivian soldiers. The battle took place in a windy little village called San Vicente high in the mountains of Bolivia.

The men robbed a payroll guard from a nearby silver mine. Besides taking a suitcase full of money, they stole one of the guard's mules. The guard saw that the outlaws were headed toward San Vicente 35 miles away.

The guard rode his other mule to a nearby police station, where he reported the crime. He offered to lead the police to San Vicente. The police agreed, even getting the assistance of a band of Bolivian soldiers.

When the payroll guard from the mine and the soldiers entered San Vicente, they spotted the stolen mule right away. Lying across the mule's back were the outlaws' ammunition and weapons.

The soldiers learned that the two outlaws were inside a hut, cooking dinner over a small oven. The soldiers surrounded the hut, and the man in charge shouted for the men inside to surrender.

But the two men did not surrender. They fired at

the soldiers, who fired back. One of the men made a run for the mule outside, heading for the ammunition and rifles. He was shot before he reached the mule but stumbled back into the hut.

The gun battle continued all evening. The next morning the soldiers cautiously approached the hut. They found one of the outlaws had died of gunshot wounds. The other had killed himself with a bullet between his eyes.

The bodies were identified as Cassidy and Sundance. The Pinkerton Agency was notified. As far as lawmen in North and South America were concerned, the days of Butch Cassidy and the Sundance Kid had ended.

BUT THEN WHO IS WILLIAM PHILLIPS?

There is an odd postscript to the violent "death" of Butch Cassidy. A man calling himself William Phillips appeared in the United States in the 1930s. Many people swear that Phillips, a businessman who worked in manufacturing and engineering, was really Butch Cassidy.

He bore a striking resemblance to the outlaw, that much no one could deny. He was recognized quickly and enthusiastically by old-timers who had known Butch. He never corrected anyone who called him by one of his outlaw names.

Yet there were others, like Phillips's wife, Gertrude, who denied that the outlaw and Phillips were the same. According to a 1938 letter to a Utah historian, Mrs. Phillips admitted that her husband knew Cassidy and had even ridden with him for a time, but he was not Cassidy.

But puzzles about William Phillips remain. He spent several months at the end of his life visiting— or revisiting—places Butch had been. In some cases, Phillips even searched some of the hiding places where some of Cassidy's loot was said to be hidden.

Phillips also visited a woman named Mary Boyd Rhodes, a former childhood sweetheart of Cassidy's. According to Rhodes's granddaughter, who was present at the meeting, Mary recognized Phillips as Cassidy. The two spent hours talking about old times. Could Mary have been mistaken about a man she had once known so well?

Another puzzling piece of evidence is a handwriting analysis done in 1974. Handwriting is often used to identify people. To a trained eye, handwriting is almost as reliable as fingerprints.

Handwriting expert Jeannine Zimmerman was given samples of both Phillips's and Cassidy's

writing. She determined that the two samples were written by the same person.

Yet there are others who scoff at the notion that Cassidy could have come back from South America. In *The Authentic Wild West,* James Horan mentioned asking Percy Seibert if he thought Cassidy might have returned. According to Horan, Seibert's answer was "Rubbish!"

Horan himself laughed at the idea that Cassidy would have—or could have—picked up a new life as a manufacturer. He found it hard to imagine that of Cassidy, a "nineteenth century cowboy with only, at most, an elementary-school education, whose greatest talent was stealing horses and robbing trains."

As for Phillips's death, it is not at all mysterious. He died of stomach cancer, in Spokane, Washington, in 1937. His family says that he was cremated and no grave exists.

You have just read the know facts about one of HISTORY'S MYSTERIES. To date, there have been no more answers to the mysteries posed in the story. There are possibilities, though. Read on and see which answer seems the most believable to you. How would you solve the case?

SOLUTIONS

▲▲▲▲▲▲▲▲▲▲▲▲▲▲▲▲▲▲▲▲▲▲▲▲▲▲▲▲▲▲

SAN VICENTE

Arthur Chapman was right in his account of Cassidy's death. After robbing the mine, Cassidy and Sundance went to the little town of San Vicente, where they died in a gun battle with local police and military. Their bodies were identified correctly. They were buried in an Indian cemetery just outside town.

WILLIAM PHILLIPS

After the mine payroll robbery, Butch and Sundance rode to San Vicente. A gun battle between Bolivian soldiers and the outlaws followed. Cassidy escaped to the outskirts of the village. His Indian friends helped him. When reports of his "death" reached him, Cassidy knew he no longer

had to fear being chased by the law. He returned to the United States. Taking the name William Phillips, he began a new life. When he died, he was cremated. His grave site will never be found.

"WRONG GUYS"

The mine payroll in Bolivia was robbed, but not by Butch Cassidy and the Sundance Kid. Two other American outlaws pulled the job, and they were shot and killed in San Vicente.

Percy Seibert used his influence in the area to see that the dead men were identified as Cassidy and Sundance. Having been friends with Cassidy, Seibert felt he owed Cassidy a chance to "go straight" without the law hounding him.

Cassidy returned to the States under another name. He wandered, visiting friends and family. Under another name, he died at his sister's ranch in Utah in 1937. His grave site is a family secret.

CLOSING THE CASE FILE

▲▲▲▲▲▲▲▲▲▲▲▲▲▲▲▲▲▲▲▲▲▲▲▲▲▲▲▲

With some mysteries, there are no leads for detectives to follow. But in the case of where and how Butch Cassidy died, there are almost too many leads. He was popular, and everyone who knew him felt they also knew the answer to his mysterious fate.

The best evidence to pinpoint Cassidy's place and time of death is his body. Pathologists are doctors who specialize in identifying human remains, even if the people have been dead for hundreds of years. But Cassidy's body has never been found.

In her book, Lula Parker Betenson wrote that the family knew where her brother was buried. She vowed to carry that secret with her to her own grave. According to her, Butch Cassidy was chased all his life, and now, in death, he is able to rest. "Where he is buried and under what name is still our secret. Revealing his burial place would furnish clues for the curious to crack that secret. I wouldn't be a Parker if I broke my word."

Too many clues, too few answers! It seems likely that the mystery of Butch Cassidy's grave site will remain unsolved.

CHRONOLOGY

▲▲

1866	April 13, Robert Leroy Parker (Butch Cassidy) is born.
1881	Robert Parker meets outlaw Mike Cassidy.
1886	Drought and hard winter hit the West.
1889	June 24, Butch Cassidy and the McCarty brothers rob a Colorado bank.
1893	July 4, Cassidy is arrested for a Wyoming horse theft.
1896	August 13, Cassidy and Wild Bunch rob an Idaho bank.
1897	April 21, Wild Bunch robs the Denver and Rio Grande Train.
1900	Wild Bunch robs a Nevada bank; later poses for photograph.
1901	Sundance and Etta Place sail for South America.
1902	Cassidy joins Sundance and Etta Place.

1908   Cassidy and Sundance reported dead after a shoot-out in San Vicente, Bolivia.

1937   William Phillips dies in Spokane, Washington.

RESOURCES

▲▲▲▲▲▲▲▲▲▲▲▲▲▲▲▲▲▲▲▲▲▲▲▲▲▲▲▲▲▲▲▲▲▲▲▲▲▲▲

SOURCES

Kelly, Charles. *Outlaw Trail: A History of Butch Cassidy and His Wild Bunch.* New York: Bonanza, 1959.

Raine, William MacLeod, and Barnes, Will C. *Cattle.* Garden City, New York: Doubleday, 1930.

FURTHER READING FOR YOUNG READERS

Collins, James L. *Lawmen of the Old West.* New York: Franklin Watts, 1990.

Lyons, Grant. *Mustangs, Six-Shooters and Barbed Wire.* New York: Julian Messner, 1981.

Surge, Frank. *Western Lawmen.* Minneapolis: Lerner, 1969.

INDEX

▲▲▲▲▲▲▲▲▲▲▲▲▲▲▲▲▲▲▲▲▲▲▲▲▲▲▲▲▲▲▲▲▲▲